MATTOTTI & KRAMSKY

DR. JEKYLL

& MR. HYDE

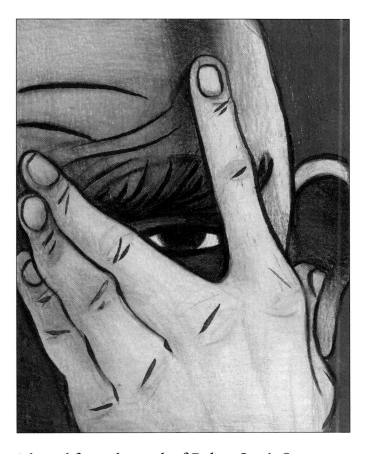

Adapted from the work of Robert Louis Stevenson

Art: Lorenzo Mattotti

Script: Lorenzo Mattotti & Jerry Kramsky

Text: Jerry Kramsky

NBM
ComicsLit

Other adaptations available from NBM:
Give It Up! and other short stories by Kafka, by Peter Kuper, $15.95
The Yellow Jar (Japanese tales), by Patrick Atangan, $12.95
The Jungle Book, by P. Craig Russell, $16.95

P&H: $3 1st item, $1 each addt'l.

We have over 150 titles,
write for our color catalog:
NBM
555 8th Ave., Suite 1202
New York, NY 10018
www.nbmpublishing.com

To Alberto Breccia
ISBN 1-56163-330-5
© 2002 Casterman
© 2002 NBM for the English translation
Translation by Adeline Darlington with extra coordination of original texts
by Jerry Kramsky and Terry Nantier, with the help of Josephine S. Richstad.
Lettering by Ortho

Printed in France
PPO Graphic, 93500 Pantin

3   2

Library of Congress Cataloging-in-Publication Data

Mattotti, Lorenzo, 1954-
  [Jekyll & Hyde. English]
  Dr. Jekyll & Mr. Hyde / Lorenzo Mattotti, Jerry Kramsky; [tranlation by Adeline
Darlington ; lettering by Ortho] ; based on the novel by Robert Louis Stevenson.
    p. cm.
  ISBN 1-56163-330-5 (hc)
    I. Title: Doctor Jekyll and Mister Hyde. II. Kramsky, Jerry. III. Darlington, Adeline.
IV. Stevenson, Robert Louis, 1850-1894. Strange case of Dr. Jekyll and Mr. Hyde. V.
Title.

PN6767.M39 J4513 2002
741.5'945--dc21

2002071922

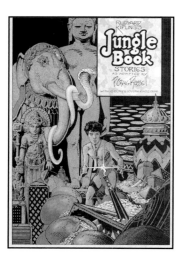

ComicsLit is an imprint
and trademark of

NANTIER ◦ BEALL ◦ MINOUSTCHINE
Publishing inc.
new york

I FEEL NOTHING BUT HORROR...

...HORROR TOWARDS THOSE LINKS OF COMMUNITY...

...WITH THAT KIND OF AN ANIMAL.

HE WILL BE OUR DOWNFALL... WE ARE JUST LIKE WILD BEASTS, WANDERING THROUGH EVER WIDER LABYRINTHS.

INNOCENT STEPS IN THE FOG.

A BODY FULL OF THE RACING ENERGY OF LIFE, IN A TRAP.

OH! WHO ARE YOU? PLEASE, LET ME THROUGH, DADDY IS NOT WELL, I MUST FETCH THE DOCTOR.

OH, WHAT A PITY... AND YOU WERE SENT OUT ALL ALONE?

OUCH! LET ME GO!

NO, YOU STAY RIGHT HERE, AND PLAY WITH ME... LET POOR HYDE PLAY!

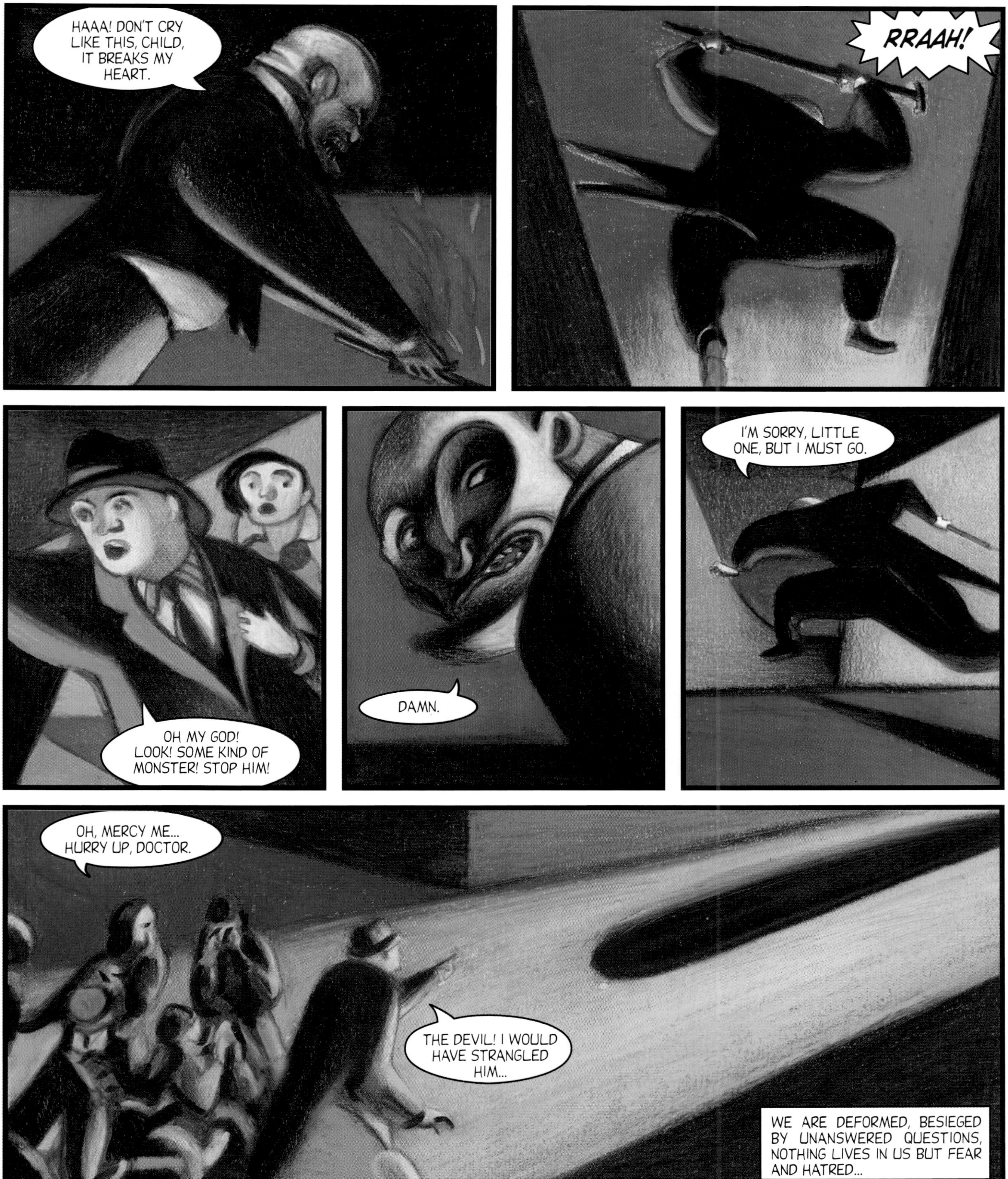
HAAA! DON'T CRY LIKE THIS, CHILD, IT BREAKS MY HEART.
RRAAH!
OH MY GOD! LOOK! SOME KIND OF MONSTER! STOP HIM!
DAMN.
I'M SORRY, LITTLE ONE, BUT I MUST GO.
OH, MERCY ME... HURRY UP, DOCTOR.
THE DEVIL! I WOULD HAVE STRANGLED HIM...
WE ARE DEFORMED, BESIEGED BY UNANSWERED QUESTIONS, NOTHING LIVES IN US BUT FEAR AND HATRED...

...AMONGST THE SLEEPY HOUSES, IN THIS UNSETTLED NIGHT,

I AM WAITING FOR YOU, DO NOT FORGET.

THIS IS POOLE SPEAKING, SIR! I HAVE A TERRIBLE INKLING! WOULD YOU COME AND SEE FOR YOURSELF?

MR. UTTERSON, THE LAWYER, WAS AWAKENED BY THE TELEPHONE.

IT WAS A WILD, COLD, SEASONABLE NIGHT OF MARCH, WITH A PALE MOON, LYING ON HER BACK AS THOUGH THE WIND HAD TILTED HER, AND FLYING WRACK OF THE MOST DIAPHANOUS AND LAWNY TEXTURE. MR. UTTERSON THOUGHT HE HAD NEVER SEEN THAT PART OF THE TOWN SO DESERTED. HE COULD HAVE WISHED IT OTHERWISE; NEVER IN HIS LIFE HAD HE BEEN CON-SCIOUS OF SO SHARP A WISH TO SEE AND TOUCH HIS FELLOW-CREA-TURES; FOR STRUGGLE AS HE MIGHT, THERE WAS BORNE IN UPON HIS MIND A CRUSHING ANTICIPATION OF CALAMITY.

WELL, SIR, HERE WE ARE, AND GOD GRANT THERE BE NOTHING WRONG.

POOLE, MY GOOD MAN! WHAT AILS YOU? IS THE DOCTOR ILL? WHAT IN GOD'S NAME ARE YOU AFRAID OF?

I HAVE BEEN AFRAID FOR SEV-ERAL DAYS, MISTER UTTERSON, SIR, THERE IS SOMETHING WRONG.

COME, COME... I CAN SEE THERE IS SOMETHING SERIOUSLY AMISS. TRY TO TELL ME WHAT IT IS.

I THINK THERE'S SOMETHING GOING ON. I THINK THERE'S BEEN FOUL PLAY.

FOUL PLAY! WHAT FOUL PLAY? WHAT DOES THE MAN MEAN?

I DAREN'T SAY, SIR, BUT NOW, SIR, COME AS GENTLY AS YOU CAN.

FOR GOD'S SAKE, POOLE...

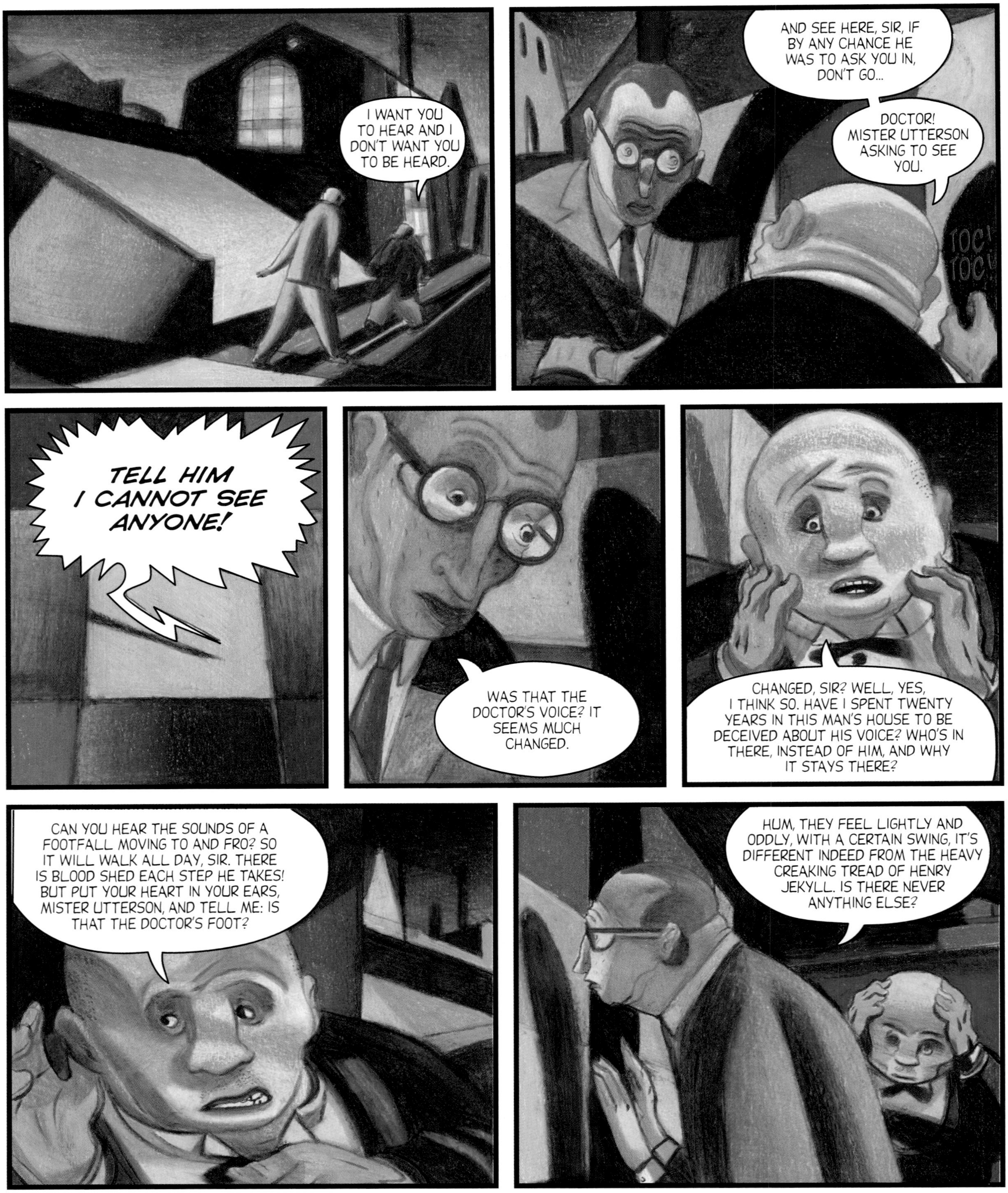
I WANT YOU TO HEAR AND I DON'T WANT YOU TO BE HEARD.
AND SEE HERE, SIR, IF BY ANY CHANCE HE WAS TO ASK YOU IN, DON'T GO...
TOC! TOC!
DOCTOR! MISTER UTTERSON ASKING TO SEE YOU.
TELL HIM I CANNOT SEE ANYONE!
WAS THAT THE DOCTOR'S VOICE? IT SEEMS MUCH CHANGED.
CHANGED, SIR? WELL, YES, I THINK SO. HAVE I SPENT TWENTY YEARS IN THIS MAN'S HOUSE TO BE DECEIVED ABOUT HIS VOICE? WHO'S IN THERE, INSTEAD OF HIM, AND WHY IT STAYS THERE?
CAN YOU HEAR THE SOUNDS OF A FOOTFALL MOVING TO AND FRO? SO IT WILL WALK ALL DAY, SIR. THERE IS BLOOD SHED EACH STEP HE TAKES! BUT PUT YOUR HEART IN YOUR EARS, MISTER UTTERSON, AND TELL ME: IS THAT THE DOCTOR'S FOOT?
HUM, THEY FEEL LIGHTLY AND ODDLY, WITH A CERTAIN SWING, IT'S DIFFERENT INDEED FROM THE HEAVY CREAKING TREAD OF HENRY JEKYLL. IS THERE NEVER ANYTHING ELSE?

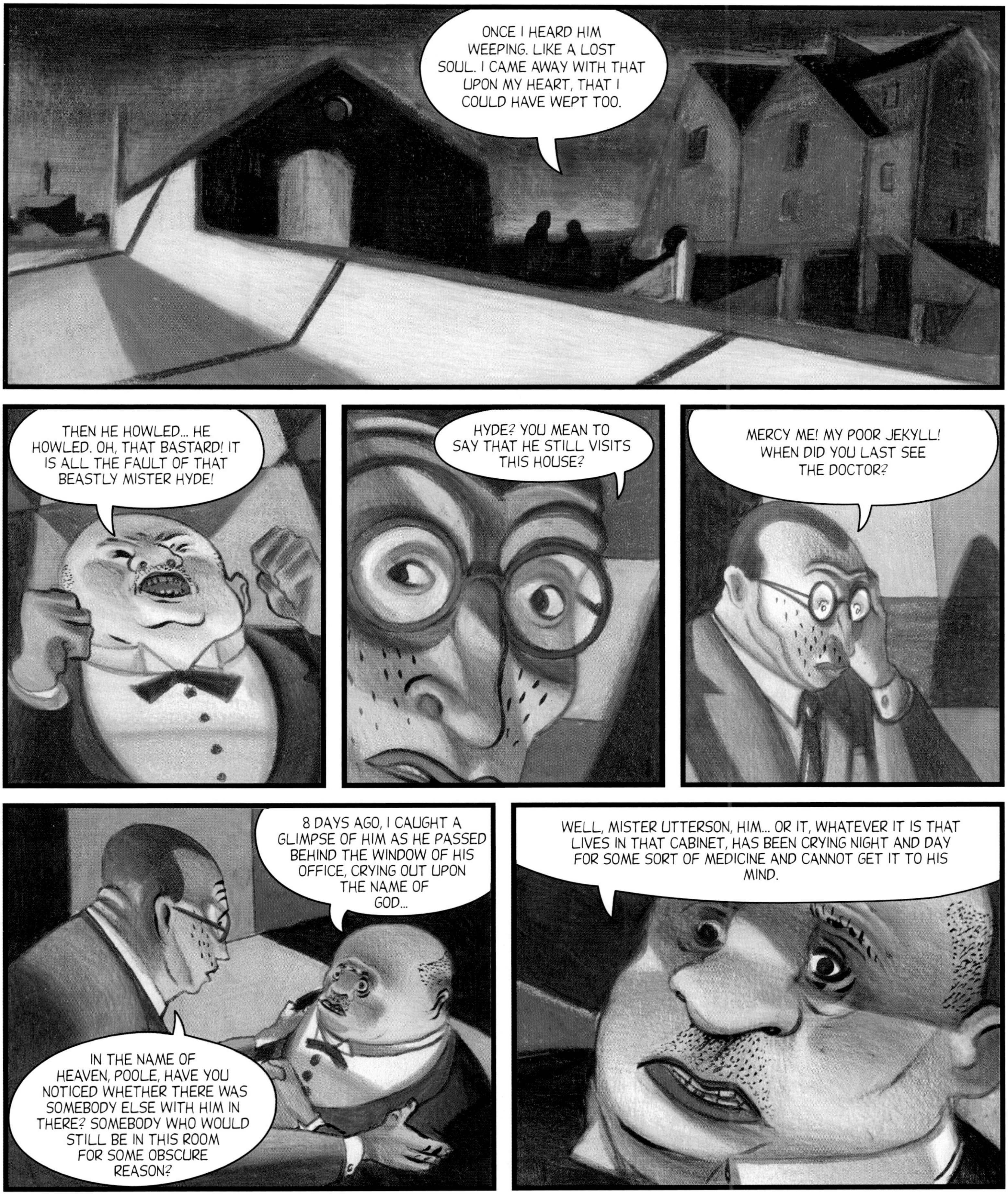
ONCE I HEARD HIM WEEPING. LIKE A LOST SOUL. I CAME AWAY WITH THAT UPON MY HEART, THAT I COULD HAVE WEPT TOO.
THEN HE HOWLED... HE HOWLED. OH, THAT BASTARD! IT IS ALL THE FAULT OF THAT BEASTLY MISTER HYDE!
HYDE? YOU MEAN TO SAY THAT HE STILL VISITS THIS HOUSE?
MERCY ME! MY POOR JEKYLL! WHEN DID YOU LAST SEE THE DOCTOR?
8 DAYS AGO, I CAUGHT A GLIMPSE OF HIM AS HE PASSED BEHIND THE WINDOW OF HIS OFFICE, CRYING OUT UPON THE NAME OF GOD...
IN THE NAME OF HEAVEN, POOLE, HAVE YOU NOTICED WHETHER THERE WAS SOMEBODY ELSE WITH HIM IN THERE? SOMEBODY WHO WOULD STILL BE IN THIS ROOM FOR SOME OBSCURE REASON?
WELL, MISTER UTTERSON, HIM... OR IT, WHATEVER IT IS THAT LIVES IN THAT CABINET, HAS BEEN CRYING NIGHT AND DAY FOR SOME SORT OF MEDICINE AND CANNOT GET IT TO HIS MIND.

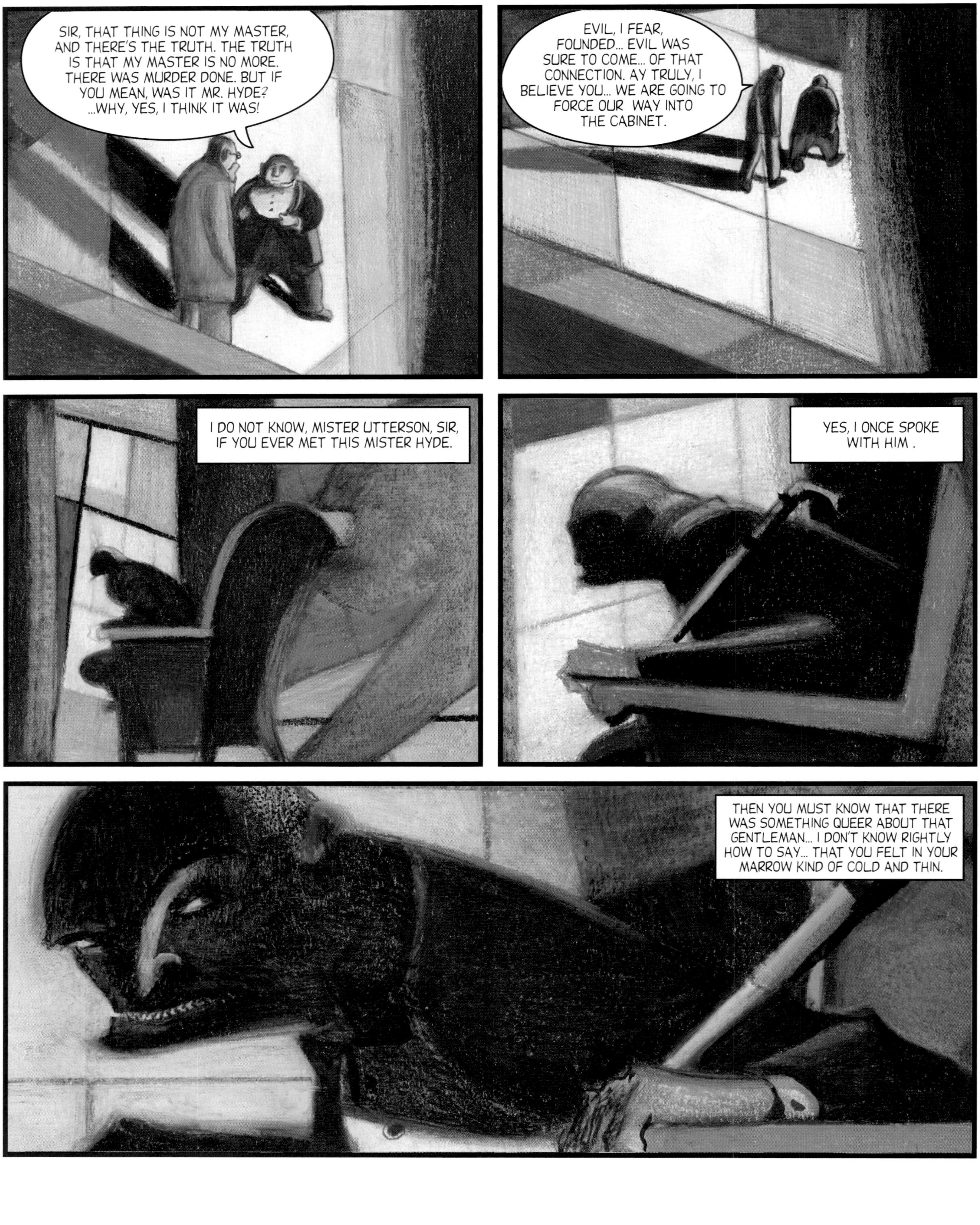
SIR, THAT THING IS NOT MY MASTER, AND THERE'S THE TRUTH. THE TRUTH IS THAT MY MASTER IS NO MORE. THERE WAS MURDER DONE. BUT IF YOU MEAN, WAS IT MR. HYDE? ...WHY, YES, I THINK IT WAS!
EVIL, I FEAR, FOUNDED... EVIL WAS SURE TO COME... OF THAT CONNECTION. AY TRULY, I BELIEVE YOU... WE ARE GOING TO FORCE OUR WAY INTO THE CABINET.
I DO NOT KNOW, MISTER UTTERSON, SIR, IF YOU EVER MET THIS MISTER HYDE.
YES, I ONCE SPOKE WITH HIM .
THEN YOU MUST KNOW THAT THERE WAS SOMETHING QUEER ABOUT THAT GENTLEMAN... I DON'T KNOW RIGHTLY HOW TO SAY... THAT YOU FELT IN YOUR MARROW KIND OF COLD AND THIN.

LET ME BE DAMNED...

...YOU MUST SUFFER ME TO GO MY OWN DARK WAY.

I HAVE BROUGHT ON MYSELF A PUNISHMENT AND A DANGER I DARE NOT NAME.

ALL THE CIRCUMSTANCES OF MY ATROCIOUS SITUATION TELL ME THAT THE END IS SURE...

...MY NAME IS HENRY JEKYLL

I WAS BORN IN THE YEAR 18- TO A LARGE FORTUNE, ENDOWED BESIDES WITH EXCELLENT PARTS. AMBITIOUS BY NATURE, I HAD EVERY GUARANTEE OF AN HONOURABLE AND DISTINGUISHED FUTURE. THE WORST OF MY FAULTS WAS A CERTAIN IMPATIENT GAIETY OF DISPOSITION I FOUND HARD TO RECONCILE WITH MY DESIRE TO WEAR A MORE THAN COMMONLY GRAVE COUNTENANCE BEFORE THE PUBLIC. HENCE IT CAME ABOUT THAT I CONCEALED MY PLEASURES FROM AN EARLY DATE, AND STOOD COMMITTED TO A PROFOUND DUPLICITY OF ME.

NOT SO FAST, JEKYLL, I DO NOT FOLLOW YOU.

MY POOR LANYON! I AM EXPLAINING TO YOU THAT I HAVE LEARNED TO RECOGNISE THE THOROUGH AND PRIMITIVE DUALITY OF MAN...

...THAT MAN IS NOT TRULY ONE, BUT TRULY TWO. I SAY TWO, BECAUSE THE STATE OF MY KNOWLEDGE DOES NOT PASS BEYOND THAT POINT.

MAN WILL BE ULTIMATELY KNOWN FOR A MERE POLITY OF MULTIFARIOUS, INCONGRUOUS AND INDEPENDENT DENIZENS.

ENOUGH HERESY, JEKYLL!

LISTEN. I HAVE LEARNED TO DWELL WITH PLEASURE, AS A BELOVED DAY-DREAM, ON THE THOUGHT OF THE SEPARATION OF THESE ELEMENTS.

IT WAS THE CURSE OF MANKIND THAT THESE INCONGRUOUS FAGGOTS WERE THUS BOUND TOGETHER- THAT IN THE AGONISED WOMB OF CONSCIOUSNESS, THESE POLAR TWINS SHOULD BE CONTINUALLY STRUGGLING.

MY FRIEND, YOU HAVE BEEN REASONING - OR RATHER LOSING YOUR REASON - IN A STRANGE WAY. YOU HAVE BECOME TOO FANCIFULL IN NURTURING SUCH UNSCIENTIFIC BALDERDASH.

LANYON, YOU DISAPPOINT ME! YOU HAVE SO LONG BEEN BOUND TO THE MOST NARROW AND TRADITIONAL VIEWS.

BE QUIET, FOR PITY'S SAKE.

THERE IS NO QUESTION OF IT! I WILL EVEN ADD THAT IF THESE ELEMENTS COULD BE HOUSED IN SEPARATE IDENTITIES, LIFE WOULD BE RELIEVED OF ALL THAT IS UNBEARABLE.

MY GOD! ALL THIS IS IMMORAL!

OH, DO NOT TALK TO ME ABOUT MORALITY! BUT JUST LOOK AROUND... GOODBYE, LANYON!

ONCE DISSOCIATED, THE UNJUST MIGHT GO HIS WAY, DELIVERED FROM THE ASPIRATIONS AND REMORSE OF HIS MORE UPRIGHT TWIN.

AND THE JUST COULD WALK ON HIS UPWARD PATH, ON WHICH HE FOUND HIS PLEASURE, NO LONGER EXPOSED TO THE DISGRACE AND PENITENCE BY THE HANDS OF HIS EXTRANEOUS EVIL.

HOW, THEN, WERE THEY DISSOCIATED? I HAD NEVER GOT CLOSER TO MY GOAL, SINCE I HAD STARTED MY TRIALS.

YOU ARE BACK, DOCTOR? I HOPE YOU'VE HAD A NICE EVENING.

THANK YOU, POOLE, YOU MAY GO TO BED. I THINK I MIGHT WORK ALL NIGHT AND I DO NOT WANT TO BE DISTURBED.

OF COURSE, SIR. I WILL SEE TO IT THAT YOU AREN'T.

CERTAIN AGENTS I HAD FOUND TO HAVE THE POWER TO SHAKE AND PLUCK BACK OUR FLESHLY VESTMENT, EVEN AS A WIND MIGHT TOSS THE CURTAINS OF A PAVILION.

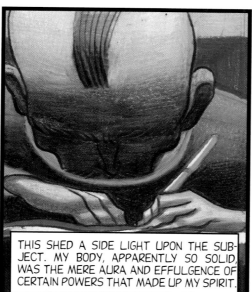

THIS SHED A SIDE LIGHT UPON THE SUBJECT. MY BODY, APPARENTLY SO SOLID, WAS THE MERE AURA AND EFFULGENCE OF CERTAIN POWERS THAT MADE UP MY SPIRIT.

THROUGH THE ADDITION OF A PARTICULAR SALT, I MANAGED TO COMPOUND A DRUG BY WHICH A SECOND FORM AND COUNTENANCE SUBSTITUTED MY NATURAL BODY, IN MY SOUL.

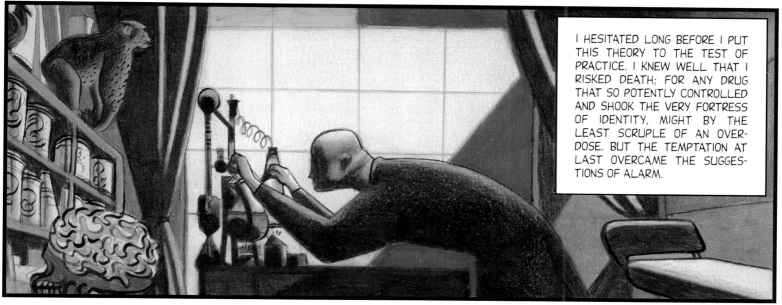

I HESITATED LONG BEFORE I PUT THIS THEORY TO THE TEST OF PRACTICE. I KNEW WELL THAT I RISKED DEATH; FOR ANY DRUG THAT SO POTENTLY CONTROLLED AND SHOOK THE VERY FORTRESS OF IDENTITY, MIGHT BY THE LEAST SCRUPLE OF AN OVERDOSE. BUT THE TEMPTATION AT LAST OVERCAME THE SUGGESTIONS OF ALARM.

LATE ONE ACCURSED NIGHT, I COMPOUNDED THE ELEMENTS INTO A POTION, AND I INJECTED IT INTO MY VEINS.

THE MOST RACKING PANGS SUCCEEDED.

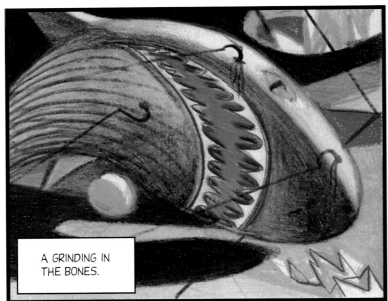

A GRINDING IN THE BONES.

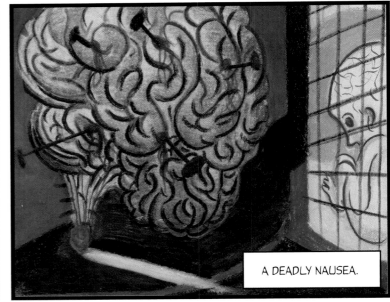

A DEADLY NAUSEA.

AND A HORROR OF THE SPIRIT THAT CANNOT BE EXCEEDED AT THE HOUR OF BIRTH OR DEATH.

MY WORST INCLINATIONS WERE LET LOOSE.

IN AMBIGUOUS SHADOWS.

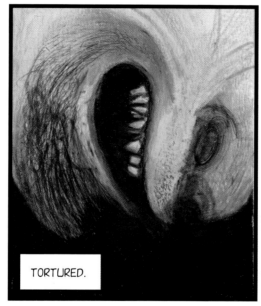

TORTURED.

THROUGH ITS STEADY PROGRESSION, EVIL HAD LEFT ON THAT BODY AN IMPRINT OF DEFORMITY AND DECAY. THEN THESE AGONIES BEGAN SWIFTLY TO SUBSIDE, AND I CAME TO MY SENSES AS IF OUT OF A GREAT SICKNESS.

HAHA... I AM SMALLER, SLIGHTER... AND YOUNGER!

WHEN I LOOKED UPON THAT UGLY IDOL IN THE MIRROR, I WAS CONSCIOUS OF NO REPUGNANCE, RATHER A LEAP OF WELCOME.

I KNEW MYSELF TO BE MORE WICKED, TENFOLD MORE WICKED; AND THE THOUGHT, IN THAT MOMENT, BRACED AND DELIGHTED ME LIKE WINE.

I STOLE THROUGH THE CORRIDORS, A STRANGER IN MY OWN HOUSE.

HA, HA... THE VERY RESPECTABLE DOCTOR JEKYLL CERTAINLY CANNOT SHOW HIMSELF LIKE THAT.

I WILL THUS BE EDWARD HYDE!!!

I CROSSED THE YARD, WHEREIN THE CONSTELLATIONS LOOKED DOWN UPON ME WITH WONDER.

IN THE STREET, I OBSERVED THAT NONE COULD COME NEAR ME AT FIRST WITHOUT A VISIBLE MISGIVING OF THE FLESH. THIS, AS I TAKE IT, WAS BECAUSE ALL HUMAN BEINGS ARE COMMINGLED OUT OF GOOD AND EVIL, AND EDWARD HYDE, ALONE IN THE RANKS OF MANKIND, WAS PURE EVIL.

THERE WAS SOMETHING STRANGE IN MY SENSATIONS, SOMETHING NEW, AND FROM ITS VERY NOVELTY, INCREDIBLY SWEET.

AAARH!!! DRINK... I AM SO THIRSTY... GIVE ME SOMETHING TO DRINK!

THE EVIL SIDE OF MY NATURE, TO WHICH I HAD NOW TRANSFERRED THE STAMPING EFFICACY, WAS LESS ROBUST AND LESS DEVELOPED THAN THE GOOD WHICH I HAD JUST DEPOSED. AFTER ALL, IT HAD BEEN MUCH LESS EXERCISED AND MUCH LESS EXHAUSTED.

PFEEE! I CAN SEE YOU, YOU BUNCH OF HYPOCRITICAL TWITS!

A CURRENT OF DISORDERED SENSUAL IMAGES WAS RUNNING LIKE A MILL RACE THROUGH MY FANCY.

FLUSHED AS I WAS WITH HOPE AND TRIUMPH, I SAVOURED WITH GREED EACH BREATH OF THIS NEW LIFE.

HEY, WHAT DOES THAT LOONY WANT?

LOUDER, YOU WEAKLING! DON'T YOU UNDERSTAND THAT TONIGHT IS THE CELEBRATION OF MY FREEDOM?

GET OUT, MIDGET!

THE DRUG HAD SHAKEN THE DOORS OF MISTER HYDE'S PRISONHOUSE: FROM NOW ON, NOBODY WOULD EVER BE ABLE TO STAND UP TO HIM.

DID YOU WISH TO MAKE FUN OF LITTLE EDWARD?

THE MORNING, BLACK AS IT WAS, WAS NEARLY RIPE FOR THE CONCEPTION OF THE DAY. THE SECOND AND CONCLUSIVE EXPERIMENT HAD YET TO BE ATTEMPTED.

IT YET REMAINED TO BE SEEN IF I HAD LOST MY IDENTITY BEYOND REDEMPTION, IN WHICH CASE I MUST FLEE BEFORE DAYLIGHT FROM THE HOUSE THAT WAS NO LONGER MINE.

I PREPARED AND INJECTED THE POTION ONCE MORE, AND ONCE MORE SUFFERED THE PANGS OF DISSOLUTION.

I CAME TO MYSELF WITH THE FACE, THE STATURE AND THE CHARACTER OF HENRY JEKYLL. EDWARD HYDE HAD PASSED AWAY LIKE A STAIN OF BREATH UPON A MIRROR.

I WISH YOU TO KNOW THAT A MISTER HYDE WILL FREQUENTLY ASSIST ME IN MY NEW AND ABSORBING RESEARCH.

HE IS OF SMALL BUILD, AND OFTEN VERY PLAINLY DRESSED. BUT ALTHOUGH HIS APPEARANCE MAY BE IMPROPER, I EXPECT YOU TO ALWAYS BE AVAILABLE FOR HIM.

FROM NOW ON, MISTER HYDE WILL HAVE FULL LIBERTY AND POWER ABOUT MY HOUSE. HE WILL THUS HAVE FREE ACCESS TO MY LABORATORY, EVEN IN MY ABSENCE.

AS YOU WISH, SIR.

ALTHOUGH GROWING TOWARDS THE ELDERLY MAN, I WOULD STILL BE MERRILY DISPOSED AT TIMES. BUT MY PLEASURES WERE, TO SAY THE LEAST, UNDIGNIFIED. IT WAS THUS ON THIS SIDE THAT MY NEW POWER TEMPTED ME. I HAD BUT TO INJECT THE POTION IN MY VEINS, TO DOFF AT ONCE THE BODY OF THE NOTED PROFESSOR, AND TO ASSUME, LIKE A THICK CLOAK, THAT OF EDWARD HYDE. THAT IS HOW I FELL IN SLAVERY.

I WAS IMMEDIATELY AWARE THAT THE EXISTENCE OF EDWARD HYDE WOULD NECESSITATE A FEW PRECAUTIONS. I MADE MY PREPARATIONS WITH THE MOST STUDIOUS CARE BY OPENING AN ACCOUNT AT ANOTHER BANK IN THE NAME OF EDWARD HYDE HIMSELF AND BY SLOPING MY OWN HAND BACKWARD. I SMILED AT THE NOTION OF RENTING OUT A ROOM, AND IT EVEN SEEMED TO ME, AT THE TIME, TO BE HUMOROUS.

MADAM, I WISH TO RENT A ROOM ON BEHALF OF A FRIEND: MISTER HYDE.

MMM, THE ONLY ONES LEFT ARE EXPENSIVE... FOLLOW ME, THE BEST ONES ARE UPSTAIRS.

MY FRIEND WISHES TO KEEP TO HIMSELF TO ATTEND TO HIS OWN AFFAIRS, WITHOUT AROUSING UNHEALTHY CURIOSITY, SO TO SPEAK...

IN THAT CASE, I WANT PAYMENT IN ADVANCE!

HYDE WAS NOT GOING TO QUIBBLE OVER THE PRICE. HE STRUCK THE DEAL FOR THAT VERY NIGHT.

YOU MAY HAVE NOTICED MY...ASSISTANTS. IF YOUR FRIEND IS INTERESTED IN ANY PARTICULAR SERVICES... AGAINST A REASONABLE TIP...

HE PAID WITHOUT A FEELING OF SHAME. BESIDES IT WAS THE BUSINESS OF A MISTER HYDE.

AS FOR ME, HENRY JEKYLL, FORTIFIED AS I SUPPOSED ON EVERY SIDE, I BEGAN TO PROFIT BY THE STRANGE IMMUNITIES OF MY POSITION. THE PLEASURES WHICH I MADE HASTE TO SEEK IN MY DISGUISE WERE UNDIGNIFIED. BUT IN THE HAND OF EDWARD HYDE, THEY WOULD SOON TURN TOWARDS THE MONSTROUS.

STOC!
STOC!
STOC!

HEY, WHO'S...?

HEH, HEH, MY NAME IS HYDE, GOOD WOMAN. I AM HERE TO TAKE POSSESSION OF MY APARTMENTS AND TO MAKE THE ACQUAINTANCE OF MY NEW LADY FRIENDS...

AN EXPRESSION THAT BORE THE STAMP OF LOWER ELEMENTS IN MY SOUL.

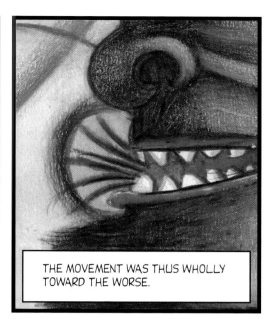

MY SECOND BODILY FORM WAS NONE THE LESS NATURAL TO ME AS THE FIRST ONE.

THE MOVEMENT WAS THUS WHOLLY TOWARD THE WORSE.

HAIEE!

STOP SQUEALING, YOU BITCH! YOU'RE MAKING ME NERVOUS!

HAHAHA! I PAY YOU, SO I WANT NO SQUEALING...

UNDER COVER OF THAT DARK NIGHT, AND OF MANY OTHERS, MY VICARIOUS DEPRAVITY BECAME MORE AND MORE UNCONTROLLABLE AND VICIOUS.

A LUSTFUL SOUL.

PERVERSE BEYOND...

EXCITEMENT...

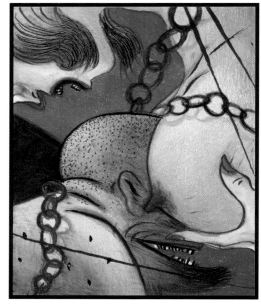

EVEN PAIN.

AAAAHH!

MEN HAVE BEFORE HIRED BRAVOS TO TRANSACT THEIR CRIMES, WHILE THEIR OWN PERSON AND REPUTATION SAT UNDER SHELTER. I WAS THE FIRST THAT EVER DID SO FOR HIS PLEASURES. I WAS THE FIRST THAT COULD THUS PLOD IN THE PUBLIC EYE WITH A LOAD OF GENIAL RESPECTABILITY, AND IN A MOMENT, STRIP OFF THESE LENDINGS AND SPRING HEADLONG INTO THE SEA OF LIBERTY. MONEY DID THE REST.

I MUST REMIND YOU, THAT MISTER UTTERSON IS EXPECTING YOU TONIGHT FOR THE MEETING AT THE CLUB... HE REQUESTED THAT I ALSO DRAW YOUR ATTENTION TO THE FACT THAT YOU HAVEN'T SEEN EACH OTHER FOR MANY WEEKS.

NO! PLEASE, POOLE, PASS ON MY DEEPEST REGRETS TO HIM FOR YET ANOTHER ABSENCE... BUT I'M AFRAID I REALLY COULDN'T, NOT TONIGHT... I AM TERRIBLY BUSY.

FAREWELL TO YOU, UTTERSON, MY FRIEND, AND TO YOU TOO, GENTLEMEN; FAREWELL TO AUSTERE LIFE AND CLEAR CONSCIENCE. INSTEAD, I WAS TRAVELLING EVER MORE AWKWARD AND LIBERATED PATHS.

CREEPING BEHIND EACH SHADOW IN THE LABORATORY, EDWARD HYDE WAS HURRYING TO COME OUT AND TAKE MY PLACE.

TO GO RUN ABOUT.

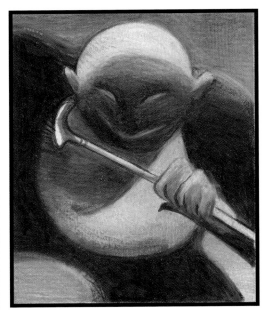

IN HIS DARK JOIE DE VIVRE.

PLEASE! SPARE A LITTLE PITY AND A LITTLE CHANGE FOR A POOR DEVIL, WHO LOST A LEG IN THAT NASTY WAR, FOR YOUR SAKE TOO!

HEY, WHY MAKE SUCH A RACKET FOR A SILLY PAIR OF LEGS! UNFORTUNATELY, I HAVE NO MONEY ON ME...

BUT POOR HYDE WILL DO SOMETHING FOR YOU ALL THE SAME... THERE YOU GO!!!

GRRR!

AH! DASTARD!

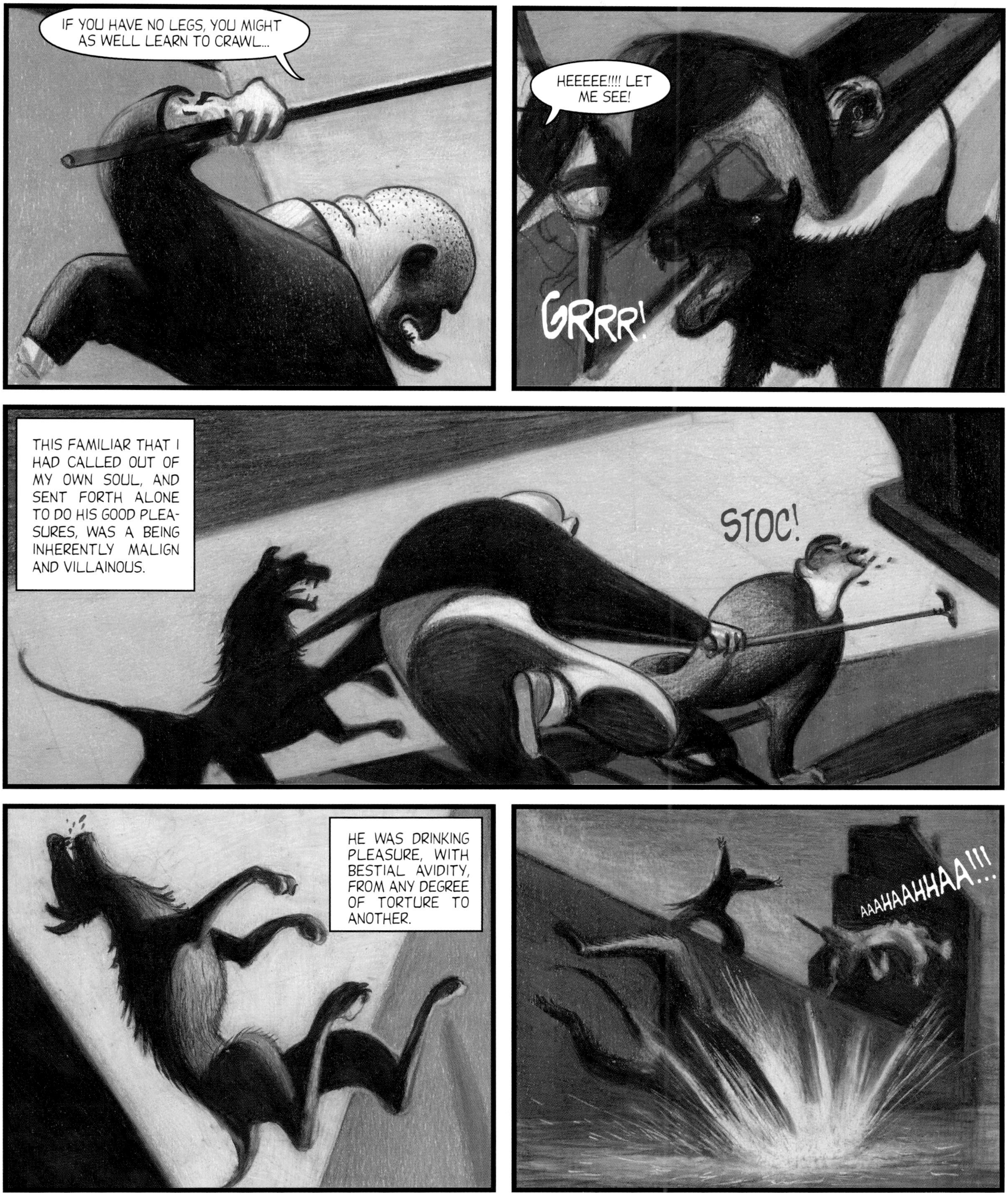
IF YOU HAVE NO LEGS, YOU MIGHT AS WELL LEARN TO CRAWL...
HEEEEE!!!! LET ME SEE!
GRRR!
THIS FAMILIAR THAT I HAD CALLED OUT OF MY OWN SOUL, AND SENT FORTH ALONE TO DO HIS GOOD PLEASURES, WAS A BEING INHERENTLY MALIGN AND VILLAINOUS.
STOC!
HE WAS DRINKING PLEASURE, WITH BESTIAL AVIDITY, FROM ANY DEGREE OF TORTURE TO ANOTHER.
AAAHAAAHHAA!!!...

RELENTLESS LIKE A MAN OF STONE.

HYDE BORE THE FACE OF A MAN WHO WAS WITHOUT BOUNDS OF MERCY. HIS MERE PRESENCE ENGENDERED A HITHER-TO UNKNOWN DISGUST, LOATHING AND FEAR, SO GREAT THAT IT WOULD BRING ABOUT NAUSEA AND DISTASTE OF LIFE.

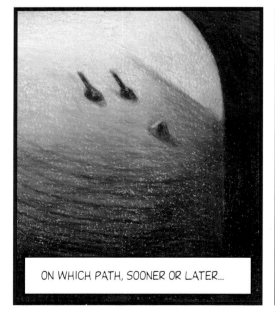

ON WHICH PATH, SOONER OR LATER...

MY CHASTISEMENT APPROACHED?

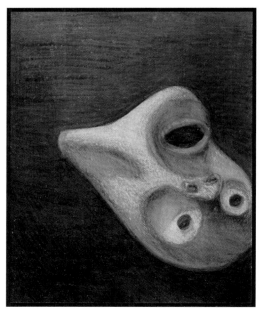

ONE DAY, I WOKE WITH SOMEWHAT ODD SENSATIONS. DROPPING BACK INTO A COMFORTABLE MORNING DOZE, A STRANGE ILLUSION STILL KEPT INSISTING THAT I WAS NOT WHERE I WAS...

GOOD MORNING, SIR.

THE ILLUSION THAT I HAD AWAKENED IN THE LITTLE ROOM OF THE DISREPUTABLE NEIGHBOURHOOD WHERE I WAS ACCUSTOMED TO SLEEP IN THE BODY OF EDWARD HYDE.

IT IS EXACTLY TEN O'CLOCK. AS YOU REQUESTED...

UNTIL THE FREEZING EVIDENCE WOKE UP IN MY BREAST AS SUDDEN AND STARTLING AS THE CRASH OF CYMBALS.

...BREAKFAST IS SERVED DOWNSTAIRS.

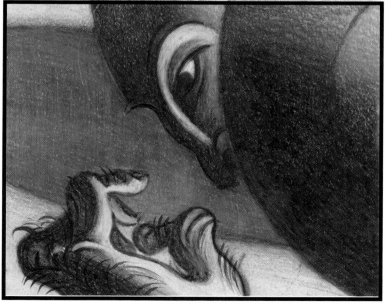

I HAD GONE TO BED JEKYLL AND I HAD AWAKENED HYDE.

IT IS A MALEFIC SIGN, AN OMEN OF CALAMITY... NO, IT IS ONLY A MISHAP, AN INEXPLICABLE ACCIDENT!

YES, BUT MISTER HYDE MUST GO, NOW... HA HA! AND HENRY JEKYLL MUST IMMEDIATELY RETURN TO HIS OWN SHAPE.

THE POWER OF THE DRUG HAD NOT BEEN ALWAYS EQUALLY DISPLAYED.

ONCE, I WAS OBLIGED TO TREBLE THE AMOUNT, WITH INFINITE RISK OF DEATH.

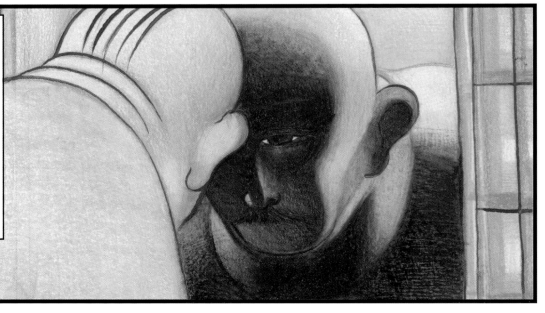

WHEREAS, IN THE BEGINNING, THE DIFFICULTY HAD BEEN TO THROW OFF THE BODY OF JEKYLL, IT HAD OF LATE GRADUALLY BUT DECIDEDLY TRANSFERRED ITSELF TO THE OTHER SIDE. I THEN BEGAN TO REFLECT MORE SERIOUSLY THAN EVER BEFORE ON THE ISSUES AND POSSIBILITIES OF MY DOUBLE EXISTENCE. IF THIS WERE MUCH PROLONGED, THE BALANCE OF MY NATURE MIGHT BE PERMANENTLY OVERTHROWN, THE POWER OF VOLUNTARY CHANGE BE FORFEITED, AND THE CHARACTER OF EDWARD HYDE BECOME IRREVOCABLY MINE. BETWEEN THESE TWO, I NOW FELT I HAD TO CHOOSE.

TO CAST IN MY LOT WITH JEKYLL, WAS TO BECOME AT A BLOW AND FOREVER, DESPISED AND FRIENDLESS.

FOR WHILE HYDE WOULD NOT BE EVEN CONSCIOUS OF ALL THAT HE HAD LOST...

...JEKYLL WOULD SUFFER SMARTINGLY IN THE FIRES OF ABSTINENCE, FROM THE LOSS OF THESE APPETITES WHICH HE HAD LONG SECRETELY INDULGED IN THE DISGUISE OF HYDE.

I WAS A TEMPTED AND TREMBLING SINNER.

CONFRONTED WITH MUCH THE SAME INDUCEMENTS AND ALARMS.

AND THEY CAST THE DIES.

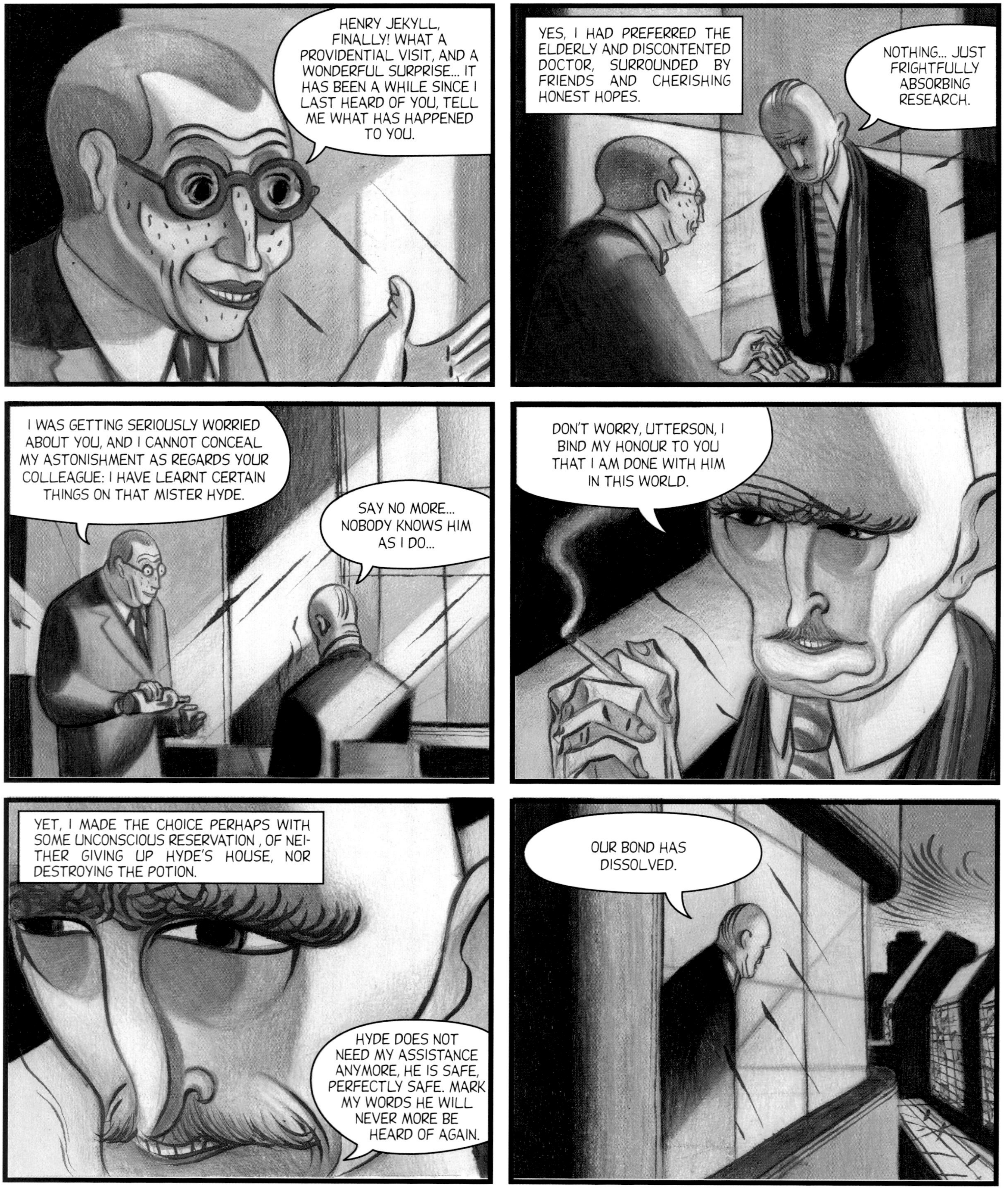
HENRY JEKYLL, FINALLY! WHAT A PROVIDENTIAL VISIT, AND A WONDERFUL SURPRISE... IT HAS BEEN A WHILE SINCE I LAST HEARD OF YOU, TELL ME WHAT HAS HAPPENED TO YOU.
YES, I HAD PREFERRED THE ELDERLY AND DISCONTENTED DOCTOR, SURROUNDED BY FRIENDS AND CHERISHING HONEST HOPES.
NOTHING... JUST FRIGHTFULLY ABSORBING RESEARCH.
I WAS GETTING SERIOUSLY WORRIED ABOUT YOU, AND I CANNOT CONCEAL MY ASTONISHMENT AS REGARDS YOUR COLLEAGUE: I HAVE LEARNT CERTAIN THINGS ON THAT MISTER HYDE.
SAY NO MORE... NOBODY KNOWS HIM AS I DO...
DON'T WORRY, UTTERSON, I BIND MY HONOUR TO YOU THAT I AM DONE WITH HIM IN THIS WORLD.
YET, I MADE THE CHOICE PERHAPS WITH SOME UNCONSCIOUS RESERVATION , OF NEITHER GIVING UP HYDE'S HOUSE, NOR DESTROYING THE POTION.
HYDE DOES NOT NEED MY ASSISTANCE ANYMORE, HE IS SAFE, PERFECTLY SAFE. MARK MY WORDS HE WILL NEVER MORE BE HEARD OF AGAIN.
OUR BOND HAS DISSOLVED.

DURING THE THREE MONTHS WHICH FOLLOWED THAT ULTIMATE AND INVOLUNTARY TRANSFORMATION, I LED A LIFE OF SUCH SEVERITY NEVER ATTAINED BEFORE. BUT TIME BEGAN AT LAST TO OBLITERATE THE FRESHNESS OF MY ALARM, AND I BEGAN TO BE TORTURED WITH THROES AND LONGINGS FOR THE MORE VOLUPTUOUS SIDE OF EXISTENCE. FOR ITS LEAPING PULSES AND SECRET PLEASURES. NOT THAT I DREAMED OF RESUSCITATING HYDE. THE BARE IDEA OF THAT WOULD STARTLE ME TO FRENZY. NO, IT WAS IN MY OWN PERSON, THAT I, HENRY JEKYLL, WAS ONCE MORE TEMPTED TO TRIFLE WITH MY CONSCIENCE.

MISTER UTTERSON, IT IS ALWAYS A PLEASURE TO SEE YOU.

I MUST SAY, POOLE, THAT I HAVE MISSED THESE OPPORTUNITIES TO REUNITE. IT HAS BEEN A WHILE SINCE THE DOCTOR LAST GAVE A GOOD PARTY.

WHAT A RELIEF TO SEE PEOPLE LIKE YOU AGAIN... WHILE SOMEONE ELSE IS BEING FOREVER KEPT AWAY FROM THIS HOUSE.

IF YOU ARE REFERRING TO THAT MISTER HYDE, I WISH YOU TO BE COMPLETELY ASSURED OF HIS DEPARTURE.

A LETTER HAS ARRIVED FROM HIM, SIR, IN WHICH HE STATES THAT HIS BENEFACTOR, DR. JEKYLL, WHOM HE HAS LONG SO UNWORTHILY REPAID FOR A THOUSAND GENEROSITIES, NEED LABOR UNDER NO ALARM FOR HIS SAFETY, AS HE HAD MEANS OF ESCAPE ON WHICH HE PLACED A SURE DEPENDENCE.

I AM DELIGHTED, POOLE.

IT LOOKS AS THOUGH OUR GOOD FRIEND HENRY JEKYLL HAS OVERDONE IT A LITTLE. WHO ARE THOSE PEOPLE WITH HIM?

HERR RUDOLPH, A NEW DIPLOMAT WHO HAS JUST REPLACED THE AMBASSADOR.

35

I KNEW ALL TOO WELL THE SIGNIFICANCE OF THAT LOOK.

I HAD LOST MYSELF. WITHIN MINUTES THAT WOMAN HAD GRAZED THE STILL TENDER SHELL I HAD BUILT FOR MY OWN DEFENCE. I COULD FEEL SOMETHING BRINGING US TOGETHER, AND IT DISTURBED ME. SOMETHING SHE HAD AWAKENED AND WHICH WAS STRUGGLING WITHIN MY SELF, SOMETHING WHICH WAS CALLED BACK FROM THOSE PROVINCES OF THE GOOD AND ILL WHICH DIVIDE AND COMPOUND MAN'S DUAL NATURE.

HEAVENS HAVE PITY UPON THAT MAN, JEKYLL! HE UTTERED SUCH CHILLING WORDS. I HOPE THAT YOU WILL AGREE WITH ME ON THAT AT LEAST!

I HAVE HEARD TOO MANY RACIAL THEORIES LATELY THAT I FIND OUTRAGEOUSLY ANTITHETIC TO OUR OATH AS DOCTORS.

LET'S LEAVE YOUR CONSIDERATIONS ON THE ETHICS OF SCIENCE ASIDE...

DON'T TAKE IT BADLY, GENTLEMEN, I MUST ADMIT RUDY KNOWS HOW TO BE UNPLEASANT, BUT YOUR DISCUSSIONS ARE USELESS. IT IS NOT UP TO HUMAN OATHS TO INFLUENCE THE COURSE OF THINGS, BUT TO THE QUIRKS OF FATE.

DESTINY! FATE! HERE COMES THE SAME OLD NONSENSE AGAIN, ADAPTED PERHAPS TO LITERATURE.

OH! OH! BEWARE: TOO MUCH DISDAIN TOWARDS CERTAIN POWERS MAY WELL TURN AGAINST YOU.

I AM SORRY, I MUST GIVE INSTRUCTIONS TO THE SERVANTS...

I NOW KNOW THAT LANYON'S FATE HAD BEEN DECIDED. AS FOR ME, THERE REMAINED EVEN FEWER WAYS OUT. I WAS MADE TO LEARN THAT THE DOOM AND BURTHEN IN OUR LIFE IS BOUND FOREVER TO MAN'S SHOULDERS, AND WHEN THE ATTEMPT IS MADE TO CAST IT OFF, IT BUT RETURNS UPON US WITH MORE UNFAMILIAR AND MORE AWFUL PRESSURE. HOWEVER, ON THAT PARTICULAR NIGHT, I WOULD TRY TO ESCAPE FROM ITS GRASP.

HENRY! DON'T YOU WANT TO DANCE?

HOW COULD I POSSIBLY HIDE UNDER MY OWN ROOF?

HOW COULD I HAVE ESCAPED FROM MYSELF?

WHY ARE YOU AVOIDING ME, HENRY? WE ARE VERY MUCH ALIKE, YOU AND I, I CAN FEEL IT. MY INSTINCT HAS NEVER FAILED ME WHEN IT COMES TO MEN...

ELDA JOINED ME IN THE STAIRCASE AND CREPT INTO MY SHADOWS. PURE BESTIAL MAGNETISM EMANATED FROM HER EYES. THE FEAR OF THE ATTRACTION THAT WOMAN AROUSED WITHIN MYSELF DREW ME EVEN CLOSER.

I LOVE DISCOVERING THE HIDDEN NATURE OF PEOPLE. WHAT ABOUT YOU?

COME, LET YOURSELF GO.

WHEN CAN WE MEET AGAIN?

I RELENTED AND AGREED TO SEE HER ON THE FOLLOWING DAY IN A DIFFERENT PART OF TOWN, ANOTHER RETREAT WHICH I SADLY KNEW TOO WELL, REQUESTING THAT SHE ASK FOR MISTER HYDE.

ELDA, WHAT ARE YOU DOING UP THERE? I WISH TO INTRODUCE YOU TO SOMEONE.

THAT MEANS THAT RUDY IS TOO TIPSY TO POUR HIS OWN DRINK... I SHALL SEE YOU TOMORROW, THEN, DOCTOR JEKYLL...

COMING, DARLING.

FROM THE STAIRCASE, I COULD WATCH PEOPLE DANCING, MERRY AND CAREFREE. AND IT IS, AS I RECALL, THE LAST IMAGE OF HARMONY THAT I RETAIN IN MY MEMORY. THAT RESPECTABLE HARMONY THAT I KNEW HOW TO JOIN, AND IN WHICH I NEVER HAD THE MORAL RESOLVE TO REMAIN.

FRAU ELDA ARRIVED FOR THE RENDEZ-VOUS WITH STUDIED TARDINESS. A HAGGED SHAFT OF DAY LIGHT GLANCED INTO THE SQUALID NEIGHBOURHOOD, STOPPING JUST BEFORE THE HOUSE, AS IF IT KNEW THE LIMITS OF ITS TERRITORY, BEYOND WHICH I WAITED FOR ELDA, TO DELVE INTO THE DEPTHS OF OUR DARKNESS TOGETHER, WITHOUT RESTRAINT.

THANKS TO MY ACUTE AND SHARPENED SENSES, I HEARD HER SPEAK WITH THE LANDLADY AND THEN ENTER. I FOLLOWED HER FOOTSTEPS IN THE STAIRCASE.

FOR THOUGH THE ONE EXPECTING HER WAS ME, THAT WAS NOT EXACTLY HENRY JEKYLL.

I AM ALL YOURS, DOCTOR JEKYLL, OR SHOULD I SAY DOCTOR HYDE?

WHERE ARE YOU HIDING, HENRY? I KNOW YOU ARE WATCHING ME.

COME, MISTER HYDE, AND COVER MY NAKED SKIN WITH PLEASURE.

ALL THIS PART OF TOWN IS MORBID AND EXCITING. IN THE STREETS, EYES WERE TRYING TO UNDRESS ME.

BUT TODAY, YOU ALONE WILL PENETRATE THE CONFINES OF MY FLESH... OF MY DESIRE...

INSTANTLY THE SPIRIT OF HELL AWOKE IN ME AND RAGED.

MY DEVIL HAD BEEN LONG CAGED.

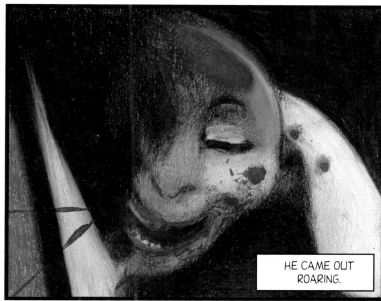

HE CAME OUT ROARING.

UNTIL THE SILENCE OF BLOOD.

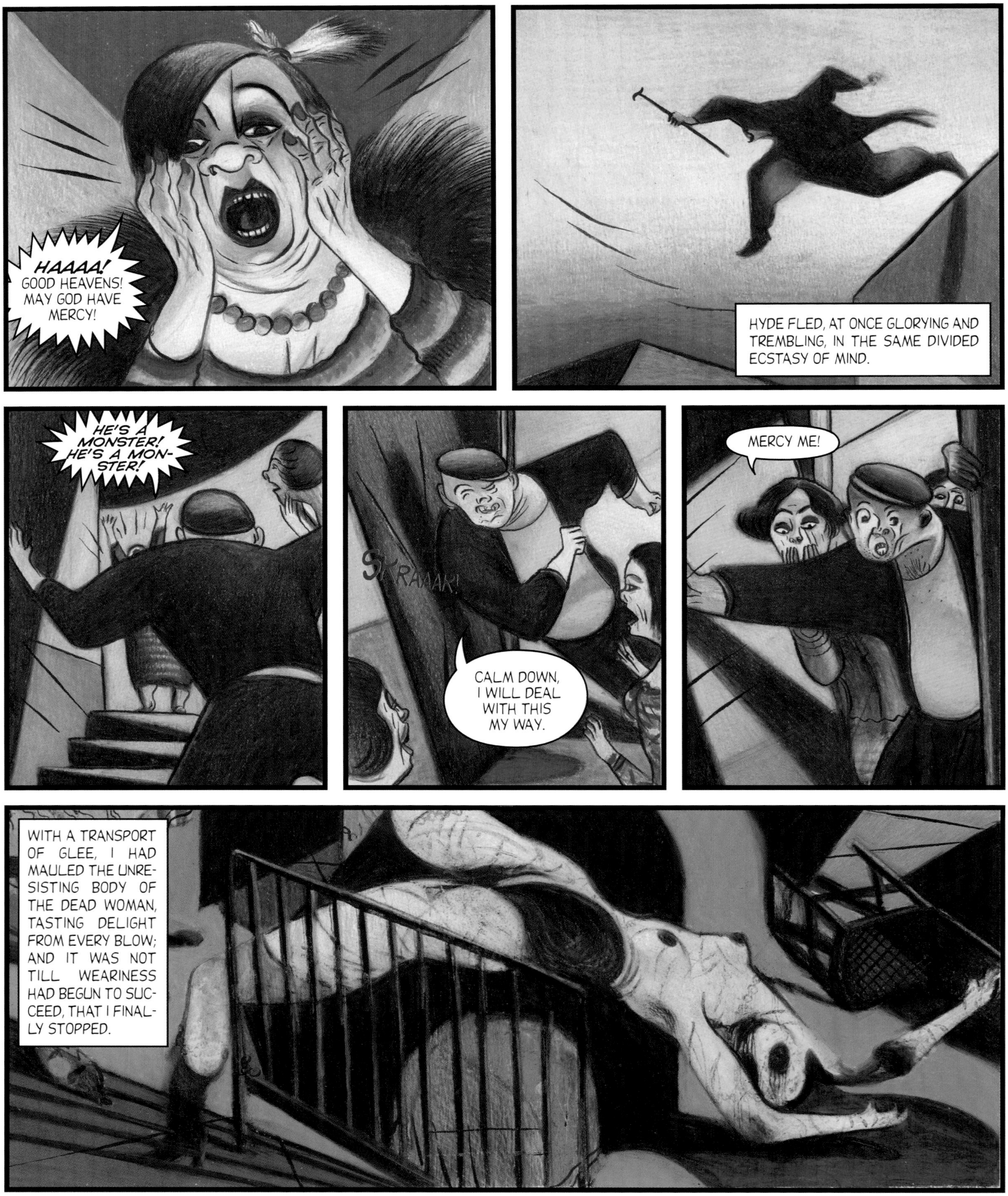

HAAAA! GOOD HEAVENS! MAY GOD HAVE MERCY!
HYDE FLED, AT ONCE GLORYING AND TREMBLING, IN THE SAME DIVIDED ECSTASY OF MIND.
HE'S A MONSTER! HE'S A MON-STER!
SKRAAAK!
CALM DOWN, I WILL DEAL WITH THIS MY WAY.
MERCY ME!
WITH A TRANSPORT OF GLEE, I HAD MAULED THE UNRE-SISTING BODY OF THE DEAD WOMAN, TASTING DELIGHT FROM EVERY BLOW; AND IT WAS NOT TILL WEARINESS HAD BEGUN TO SUC-CEED, THAT I FINAL-LY STOPPED.

MY GUILT WAS PATENT TO THE WORLD, AND THE VICTIM WAS A PERSON HIGH IN PUBLIC ESTIMATION: THE WIFE OF A DIPLOMAT. IT WAS NOT ONLY A CRIME, BUT A TRAGIC FOLLY.

I RAN TO THE LABORATORY. JEKYLL WAS NOW MY REFUGE OF MERCY.

I DESPERATELY NEEDED TO TRANSFORM AGAIN.

HEAVENS! MISTER HYDE!

STEP BACK, RASCAL, YOUR MASTER NEEDS ME ONE LAST TIME!

HYDE WAS THENCEFORTH IMPOSSIBLE.

ALL I WANTED WAS TO HASTEN THE TRANSFORMATION.

HELL AND DAMNATION!

CR
CRUNCH

HELL! THE MAIN INGREDIENT HAS MIXED WITH THE OTHER SUBSTANCES.

I MUST FIND SOME MORE... QUICKLY... I MUST PREPARE ANOTHER DOSE...

YES, CONSTABLE, SOMEBODY HAS BROKEN INTO THE DOCTOR'S CONSULTING ROOM... SEND OVER SOME MEN, I FEAR FOR MY OWN SAFETY.

HIS LUST OF EVIL GRATIFIED AND STIMULATED, HIS LOVE OF LIFE SCREWED TO THE TOPMOST PEG, HYDE RAN TO THE PHARMACY, HEARKENING IN HIS WAKE FOR THE STEPS OF THE AVENGER.

SORRY, WE'RE CLOSED. COME BACK TOMORROW.

NO, I MUST HAVE THIS SALT NOW! IT IS FOR DOCTOR JEKYLL.

I REMEMBER YOU, NOW... THE DOCTOR IS A REGULAR CUSTOMER TO OUR PHARMACY. LET'S SEE UP HERE... PHOSPHORUS, VOLATILE ETHERS, CRYSTALLINE SALTS, HERE IT IS.

IT COMES FROM A NEW SUPPLIER, IT IS SLIGHTLY MORE EXPENSIVE.

HURRY! HURRY!

PLEASE TELL YOUR MASTER PAYMENT IS NO URGENT MATTER.

GIVE ME THAT! I AM A SERVANT TO NO ONE. I SPEND THE MONEY THAT I WANT AND I DO WHAT I LIKE.

EDWARD HYDE RAGED AT THE MERE THOUGHT THAT, NOW, WHETHER HE WOULD OR NOT, HE WOULD HAVE TO EMBRACE ANEW THE RESTRICTIONS OF NATURAL LIFE, THAT OF HENRY JEKYLL'S.

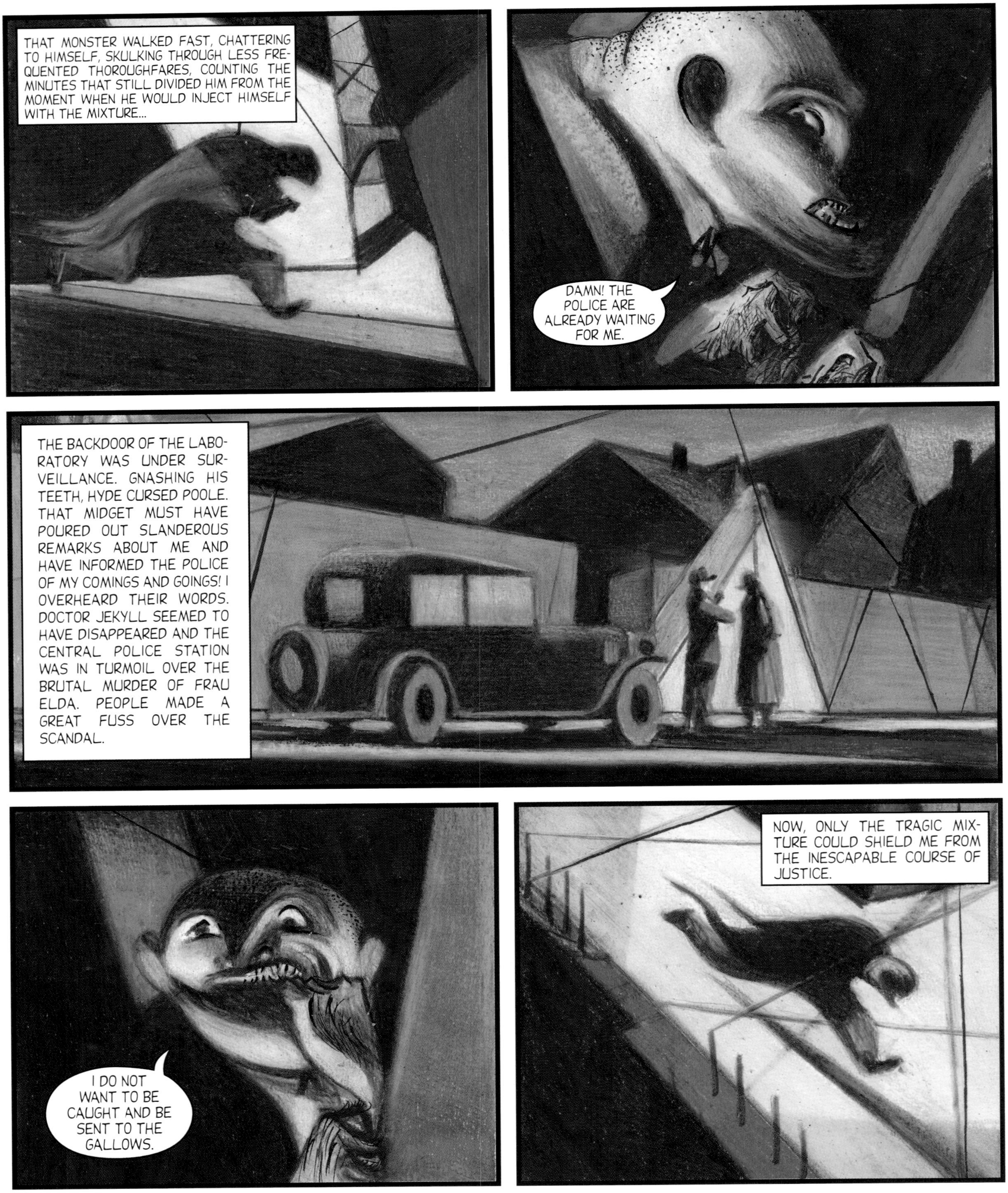
THAT MONSTER WALKED FAST, CHATTERING TO HIMSELF, SKULKING THROUGH LESS FREQUENTED THOROUGHFARES, COUNTING THE MINUTES THAT STILL DIVIDED HIM FROM THE MOMENT WHEN HE WOULD INJECT HIMSELF WITH THE MIXTURE...
DAMN! THE POLICE ARE ALREADY WAITING FOR ME.
THE BACKDOOR OF THE LABORATORY WAS UNDER SURVEILLANCE. GNASHING HIS TEETH, HYDE CURSED POOLE. THAT MIDGET MUST HAVE POURED OUT SLANDEROUS REMARKS ABOUT ME AND HAVE INFORMED THE POLICE OF MY COMINGS AND GOINGS! I OVERHEARD THEIR WORDS. DOCTOR JEKYLL SEEMED TO HAVE DISAPPEARED AND THE CENTRAL POLICE STATION WAS IN TURMOIL OVER THE BRUTAL MURDER OF FRAU ELDA. PEOPLE MADE A GREAT FUSS OVER THE SCANDAL.
I DO NOT WANT TO BE CAUGHT AND BE SENT TO THE GALLOWS.
NOW, ONLY THE TRAGIC MIXTURE COULD SHIELD ME FROM THE INESCAPABLE COURSE OF JUSTICE.

WITHIN THE CONFUSION OF THE LABORATORY, I HAD INSTINCTIVELY PICKED UP A SYRINGE AND TEST TUBES. IT NOW REMAINED FOR ME TO FIND AN ISOLATED PLACE, AND THANKS TO THAT MAKESHIFT EQUIPMENT, PREPARE THE POTION.

THOSE WRETCHES WILL NOT HAVE ME... I KNOW FULL WELL HOW TO FOOL THEM.

IT'S CHILD'S PLAY.

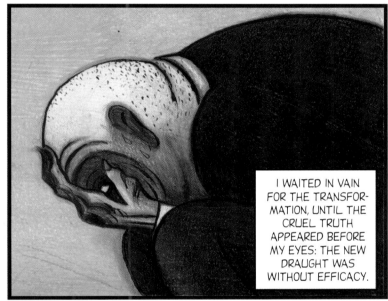

I WAITED IN VAIN FOR THE TRANSFORMATION, UNTIL THE CRUEL TRUTH APPEARED BEFORE MY EYES: THE NEW DRAUGHT WAS WITHOUT EFFICACY.

MY REASON WAVERED.

HYDE IN DANGER OF HIS LIFE WAS A NEW CREATURE TO ME. HE DISPLAYED UNEXPECTED RESOURCES. WHERE JEKYLL PERHAPS MIGHT HAVE SUCCUMBED, HYDE WAS ASTUTE AND MASTERED HIMSELF.

THEN I REMEMBERED THAT OF MY ORIGINAL CHARACTER, ONE PART REMAINED TO ME: I COULD WRITE MY OWN HAND. I THUS COMPOSED AN IMPORTANT LETTER, IN WHICH I REQUESTED LANYON TO ANALYSE A PARTICULAR SALT.

"DEAR LANYON, MY LIFE AND REASON ARE AT YOUR MERCY. AT MIDNIGHT, I ASK YOU TO SEE A PERSON, IN YOUR CONSULTING ROOM, A MAN WHO WILL PRESENT HIMSELF IN MY NAME TO HAND YOU THE ABOVE MENTIONED SUBSTANCE. I AM CONFIDENT THAT ALL WILL BE SETTLED AS IN THE END OF A BAD DREAM. PLEASE HELP ME AND SAVE YOUR FRIEND H.J."

DON'T LOSE IT OR YOU WILL BE SORRY.

YES, SS... SIR.

I WAITED IN THE BACKGROUND, WITH THE RELENTLESS HORROR OF POTENTIALLY GREATER COMPLICATIONS.

FINALLY, I WENT TO THE MEETING, AN UNKNOWN AND DISPLEASING VISITOR.

DOCTOR LANYON ENJOYED LINGERING AT HIS CONSULTING ROOM, METICULOUSLY DOUBLE-CHECKING THE DAY'S WORK.

AHRR, LANYON, DOCTOR LANYON! YOU MUST HAVE READ THE MESSAGE, SO YOU KNOW WHAT REMAINS FOR YOU TO DO.

MY GOD! WHO ARE YOU?

HOW CAN HENRY JEKYLL USE SOMEONE LIKE YOU, AND SEND YOU TO ME PRECEDED BY A DELIRIOUS LETTER? HE MUST BE INSANE.

LET'S SAY I AM A COLLABORATOR OF THE DOCTOR'S... WHOM JEKYLL CANNOT POSSIBLY DISREGARD.

MMM, IT LOOKS LIKE QUITE ORDINARY CHLORIDE OF...

GO ON! DECOMPOSE IT WITH A SOLVENT... OR THROUGH ELECTROLYSIS...

DAMN!!! I DECIDE WHAT MUST BE DONE!

LANYON PROCEEDED WITH METICULOUS COMPOSURE. THAT MERE WAIT WAS TORTURE TO HYDE. HIS APELIKE MIND BEGAN TO GROWL FOR LICENSE. LIKE A WILD BEAST ISOLATED FROM ITS TERRITORY, HE NESTLED, AS IF LOST, OUT OF THE WAY, ON THE BRINK OF DEEPEST AND DARKEST DESPAIR.

WELL, IT IS EXACTLY WHAT I HAD SUPPOSED: A MORE THAN USUAL CRYSTALLISATION. PURE BICHLORIDE OF...

PURE! DAMN! HOW CAN IT BE PURE? HOW IS IT, THEN, THAT IT IS INEFFECTIVE?

GOOD HEAVENS! WHAT ARE YOU MUTTERING ABOUT? WHAT SHOULD BE DONE?

ALLOW JEKYLL TO COME BACK! IDIOT!!! WHAT ELSE!?

HOW DARE YOU... YOUR MADNESS GOES TOO FAR.

ENOUGH! GET OUT! IMMEDIATELY! I WANT NOTHING TO DO WITH YOU!

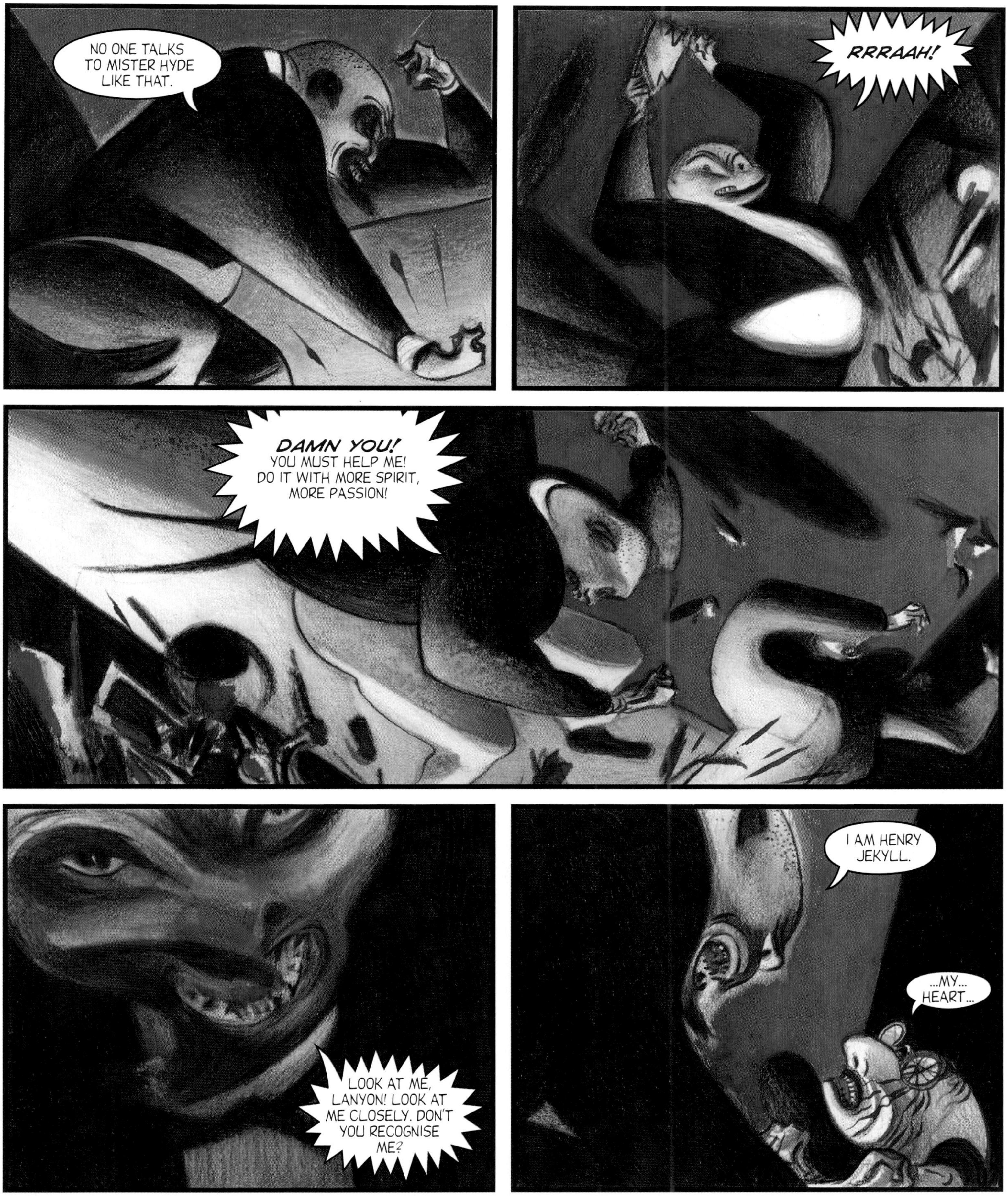
NO ONE TALKS TO MISTER HYDE LIKE THAT.
RRRAAH!
DAMN YOU! YOU MUST HELP ME! DO IT WITH MORE SPIRIT, MORE PASSION!
LOOK AT ME, LANYON! LOOK AT ME CLOSELY. DON'T YOU RECOGNISE ME?
I AM HENRY JEKYLL.
...MY... HEART...

WHEN LANYON STOPPED BREATHING, I STAYED AND WATCHED HIS MISERABLE AND MOTIONLESS FACE ON THE GROUND, DIVIDED BETWEEN JOY AND DISGUST. THERE REMAINED NOTHING IN HIS CONSULTING ROOM THAT I HAD NOT BROKEN. THEN, THE LIGHT OF DAWN DROVE ME AWAY. I BEGAN WANDERING WITH NEITHER REST NOR AIM, HUGGING THE WALLS.

THE NIGHT BEFORE, I HAD BEEN SAFE OF ALL MEN'S RESPECT, WEALTHY, BELOVED.

NOW I WAS NOTHING BUT AN OUTLAW.

FOREVER, DESPISED BY MY PEERS.

NOW AND FOREVER A PRISONER TO MY EVIL SOUL.

THE HANDS OF ALL MEN WOULD BE RAISED TO TAKE AND SLAY ME.

RELEGATED TO THE SOCIETY OF GROTESQUE BEINGS, ALL READY TO ABUSE MY SLIGHTEST WEAKNESS. FROM NOW ON, ALONE, WITHOUT THE ASSISTANCE OF DOCTOR JEKYLL. FEELING, ON THE CONTRARY, PROFOUND AVERSION AND POWERLESS HATRED TOWARDS THAT OTHER PART OF MY SELF.

FOUL-SMELLING SHADOWS WILL BE A MEAN BED TO ME.

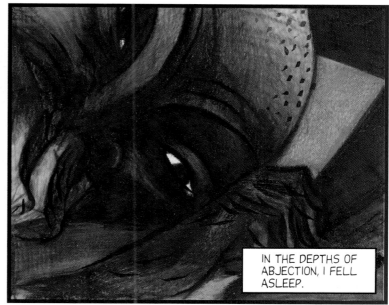

IN THE DEPTHS OF ABJECTION, I FELL ASLEEP.

WITH A STRINGENT AND PROFOUND SLUMBER.

CONTINUALLY VISITED BY A MACABRE DANCE.

I SOUGHT IN VAIN WITH TEARS AND PRAYERS TO SMOTHER DOWN THE CROWD OF HIDEOUS IMAGES AND SOUNDS WITH WHICH MY MEMORY SWARMED AGAINST ME.

BETWEEN MY PETITIONS, THEY MOVED IN CLOSER YET.

AND THE UGLY FACE OF MY INIQUITY STARED INTO MY SOUL.

OH!... THANK YOU, DADDY.

THE VEIL OF SELF-INDUL-GENCE WAS RENT FROM HEAD TO FOOT, I SAW MY LIFE AS A WHOLE: I FOLLOWED IT UP FROM THE DAYS OF CHILD-HOOD, WHEN I WALKED WITH MY FATHER'S HAND.

YOU KNOW HOW MUCH I LIKE GOLDFISH.

THIS SENSE OF JOY, WHICH I THOUGHT STAINLESS, ALREADY MARKED WITH ANGUISH.

WHICH THEN TURNED INTO THE SELF-DENYING TOILS...

...OF MY PROFESSIONAL LIFE.

I WOKE HENRY JEKYLL.

I SAW LANYON'S DEATH PARTLY IN A DREAM, AND IT WAS PARTLY IN A DREAM THAT I CAME HOME TO MY OWN HOUSE.

DOCTOR! THE STATE OF YOU! WHERE HAVE YOU BEEN THESE TWO DAYS?

EVERYTHING WAS SHROUDED IN THE SAME VAGUE SENSATION.

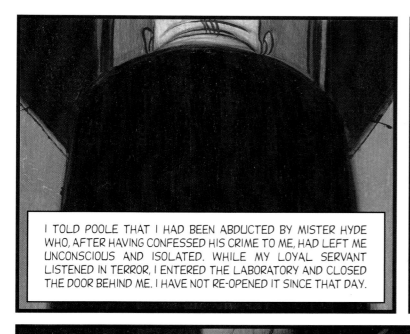

I TOLD POOLE THAT I HAD BEEN ABDUCTED BY MISTER HYDE WHO, AFTER HAVING CONFESSED HIS CRIME TO ME, HAD LEFT ME UNCONSCIOUS AND ISOLATED. WHILE MY LOYAL SERVANT LISTENED IN TERROR, I ENTERED THE LABORATORY AND CLOSED THE DOOR BEHIND ME. I HAVE NOT RE-OPENED IT SINCE THAT DAY.

FROM THAT DAY FORTH IT SEEMED ONLY BY A GREAT EFFORT AS OF GYMNASTICS, AND ONLY WHEN I TRIED AND TRIED THE MIXTURE AGAIN, IN DIFFERENT DOSES, THAT I WAS ABLE TO WEAR THE COUNTENANCE OF JEKYLL.

AT ALL HOURS OF THE DAY AND NIGHT, I WOULD BE TAKEN WITH THE PREMONITORY SHUDDER. IN VAIN DID I SEND POOLE ACROSS THE TOWN IN SEARCH OF THE SALT. I AM NOW PERSUADED THAT MY FIRST SUPPLY WAS IMPURE, AND THAT IT WAS THAT UNKNOWN IMPURITY WHICH LENT EFFICACY TO THE DRAUGHT. IT WOULD NOT BE LONG BEFORE I WOULD PART WITH MY ORIGINAL APPEARANCE.

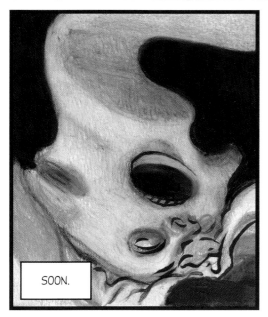

SOON.

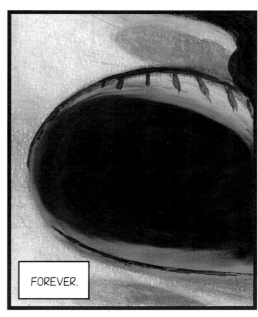

FOREVER.

THERE ONLY REMAINED ONE AND ONLY HOPE.

I SHOULD CLING TO THE PUREST MEMORIES.

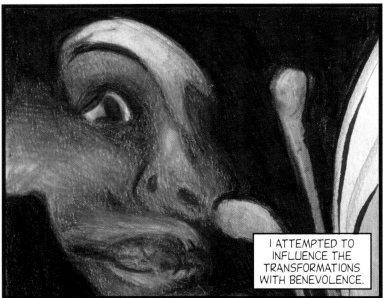

I ATTEMPTED TO INFLUENCE THE TRANSFORMATIONS WITH BENEVOLENCE.

I HAD FLOWERS AND AN AQUARIUM DELIVERED.

ABOVE ALL, I KNEW THAT IF I SLEPT OR EVEN DOZED FOR A MOMENT, IT WAS ALWAYS AS HYDE THAT I AWAKENED. UNDER THE STRAIN OF THIS CONTINUALLY IMPENDING DOOM AND BY THE SLEEPLESSNESS TO WHICH I NOW CONDEMNED MYSELF, EVEN BEYOND WHAT I HAD THOUGHT POSSIBLE TO MAN, I BECAME, IN MY OWN PERSON, A CREATURE EATEN UP AND EMPTIED BY FEVER, LANGUIDLY WEAK BOTH IN BODY AND MIND, AND SOLELY OCCUPIED BY ONE THOUGHT: THE HORROR OF MY OTHER SELF.

DO NOT THINK THAT I DON'T KNOW, JEKYLL! YOU ARE THINKING OF LIBERATING YOURSELF FROM ME THROUGH SUICIDE, BUT I WILL NOT LET YOU. I WILL NOT GIVE YOU THE TIME TO DO IT.

WHEN HYDE SLEPT, HIS FANCY WOULD BE BRIMMING WITH IMAGES OF TERROR, A SOUL BOILING WITH CAUSE-LESS HATRED. HE LIVED CONSUMED BY RAGE AND FROZEN BY FEARS.

YOUR FISH WILL DIE FIRST.

YOUR FLOWERS WILL WILT.

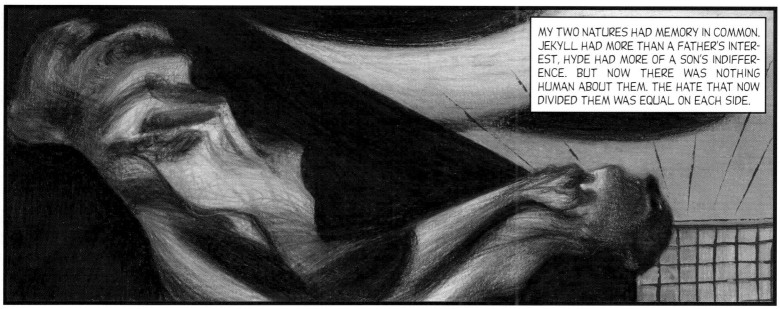

MY TWO NATURES HAD MEMORY IN COMMON. JEKYLL HAD MORE THAN A FATHER'S INTER-EST, HYDE HAD MORE OF A SON'S INDIFFER-ENCE. BUT NOW THERE WAS NOTHING HUMAN ABOUT THEM. THE HATE THAT NOW DIVIDED THEM WAS EQUAL ON EACH SIDE.

AS I RECALL HYDE'S ABJECTION, I WOULD FEEL A HORRID NAUSEA AND THE MOST DEADLY SHUDDERING, AND YET, AS I SAW HIS WONDERFUL LOVE OF LIFE, HOW HE FEARED MY POWER TO CUT HIM OFF BY SUICIDE, I FOUND IT IN MY HEART TO PITY HIM.

THE SKY... THE CLOUDS... BRING MEAGRE COMFORT TO ME...THIS, THEN, IS THE LAST TIME, SHORT OF A MIRACLE, THAT HENRY JEKYLL CAN THINK HIS OWN THOUGHTS.

THERE COMES AN END TO ALL THINGS. THE MOST CAPACIOUS MEASURE IS FILLED AT LAST.

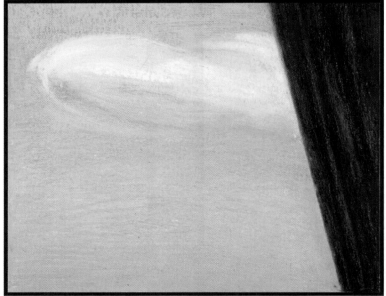

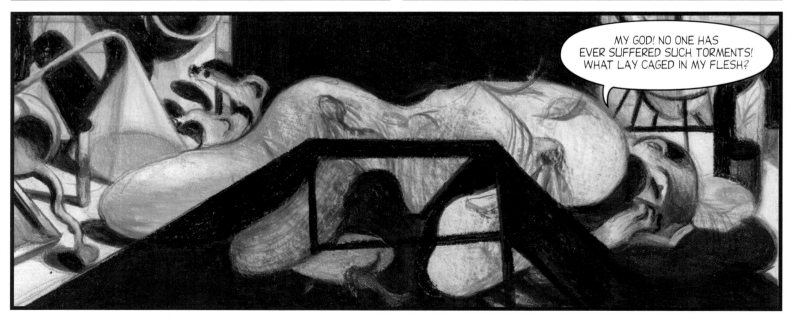

MY GOD! NO ONE HAS EVER SUFFERED SUCH TORMENTS! WHAT LAY CAGED IN MY FLESH?

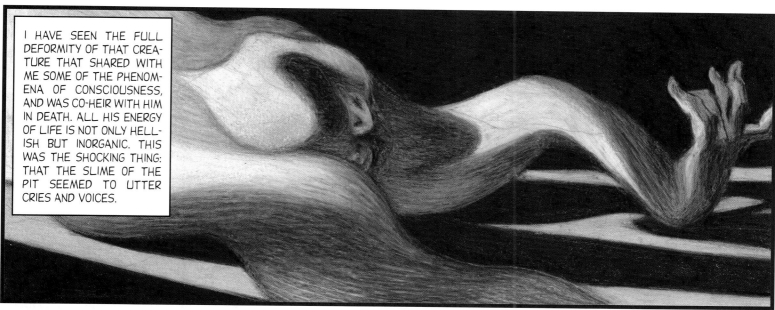

I HAVE SEEN THE FULL DEFORMITY OF THAT CREATURE THAT SHARED WITH ME SOME OF THE PHENOMENA OF CONSCIOUSNESS, AND WAS CO-HEIR WITH HIM IN DEATH. ALL HIS ENERGY OF LIFE IS NOT ONLY HELLISH BUT INORGANIC. THIS WAS THE SHOCKING THING: THAT THE SLIME OF THE PIT SEEMED TO UTTER CRIES AND VOICES.

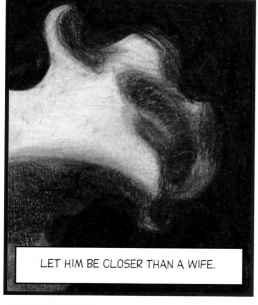

LET HIM BE CLOSER THAN A WIFE.

CLOSER THAN AN EYE.

THIS IS MY TRUE HOUR OF DEATH. AND WHAT IS TO FOLLOW CONCERNS ANOTHER THAN MYSELF.

JEKYLL! I DEMAND TO SEE YOU AND I WILL, IF NOT BY FAIR MEANS, THEN BY FOUL...DOWN WITH THE FOOR, MR. FULLER!!!

SKRAAAK!

AAAHAA!

HOLD ON! MAY GOD BE WITH YOU...

IT'S HORRIBLE... HORRIBLE...IT SOUNDS LIKE THE CRY OF A TERRORIZED ANIMAL.

THE WOOD WAS TOUGH AND THE FITTINGS WERE OF EXCELLENT WORKMANSHIP; AND IT WAS NOT UNTIL THE FIFTH BLOW THAT THE WRECK OF THE DOOR FELL. THE BESIEGERS, APPALLED BY THEIR OWN RIOT AND THE STILLNESS THAT HAD SUCCEEDED, PEERED IN. RIGHT IN THE MIDDLE THERE LAY THE BODY OF A MAN SORELY CONTORTED AND STILL TWITCHING. THE CORDS OF HIS FACE STILL MOVED WITH A SEMBLANCE OF LIFE, BUT LIFE WAS QUITE GONE: AND BY THE CRUSHED PHIAL IN THE HAND AND THE STRONG SMELL OF KERNELS THAT HUNG UPON THE AIR, UTTERSON KNEW THAT HE WAS LOOKING ON THE BODY OF A SELF-DESTROYER.